W9-BMP-416

Arduino

CHERRY LAKE PUBLISHING • ANN ARBOR, MICHIGAN

by Terence O'Neill and Josh Williams

CHERRY LAKE
Publishing

A Note to Adults: Please review the instructions for the activities in this book before allowing children to do them. Be sure to help them with any activities you do not think they can safely complete on their own.

A Note to Kids: Be sure to ask an adult for help with these activities when you need it. Always put your safety first!

Published in the United States of America by Cherry Lake Publishing
Ann Arbor, Michigan
www.cherrylakepublishing.com

Series Editor: Kristin Fontichiaro
Photo Credits: Cover and page 1, ©ZUMA Press, Inc./Alamy; page 4, ©dam/www.flickr.com/CC-BY-2.0; page 5, ©adactio/www.flickr.com/CC-BY-2.0; page 6, ©decoded_conf/www.flickr.com/CC-BY-2.0; pages 7, 17, and 28, courtesy of Michigan Makers; page 9, ©John Loo/www.flickr.com/CC-BY-2.0; page 10, ©KathyReid/www.flickr.com/CC-BY-2.0; page 12, ©Beckathwia/www.flickr.com/CC-BY-SA-2.0; page 15, ©g.p.macklin/www.flickr.com/CC-BY-SA-2.0; page 19, ©indy138/www.flickr.com/CC-BY-SA-2.0; page 25, ©zappowbang/www.flickr.com/CC-BY-2.0; page 27, ©dvanzuijlekom/www.flickr.com/CC-BY-SA-2.0

Library of Congress Cataloging-in-Publication Data
O'Neill, Terence, 1984–
  Arduino/by Terence O'Neill and Josh Williams.
     pages cm.—(Makers as innovators) (Innovation library)
  Audience: Grade 4 to 6.
  Includes bibliographical references and index.
  ISBN 978-1-62431-137-6 (library binding)—ISBN 978-1-62431-269-4 (paperback)—ISBN 978-1-62431-203-8 (e-book)
  1. Arduino (Microcontroller)—Juvenile literature. 2. Arduino (Microcontroller)—Programming—Juvenile literature. I. Williams, Josh, 1981– II. Title.
  TJ223.P76054 2013
  629.8'955133—dc23   2013004927

Cherry Lake Publishing would like to acknowledge the work of The Partnership for 21st Century Skills. Please visit *www.p21.org* for more information.

Printed in the United States of America
Corporate Graphics Inc.
July 2013
CLFA13

Contents

Chapter 1

Meet the Arduino

Have you ever wanted to make a robot? Would you like to create an interactive light show? Do you want to turn your idea for an amazing invention into reality? Then the Arduino microcontroller is for you! A microcontroller is a simple computer that passes information between **hardware** and **software**. Let's say you have trouble waking up in the morning. You could use an Arduino to sense when the sun comes up. When the Arduino senses light, it triggers a speaker to make noise. In this example, the hardware is a light sensor

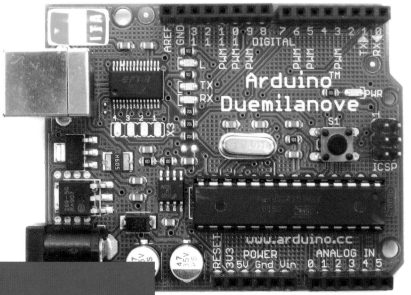

An Arduino is roughly the size of a credit card.

Controlling a light is just one of the many things an Arduino can be programmed to do.

and a speaker. The software is the instructions sent to the Arduino that tell it to take **input** from the sensor and send **output** to the speaker.

The Arduino makes it easier for **makers** to turn ideas into working products. This book will introduce the basics of the Arduino. As you read, it will be help-ful if you have access to the Internet and the Arduino

Inventing Arduino

Many inventions begin when someone sees that there is a need to be filled or a problem to be solved. What was the challenge that led to the Arduino? Students at the Interaction Design Institute Ivrea in Italy needed to design products and inventions. Creating the computer "brain" to run these inventions was taking too much time and money. What if there was an inexpensive way to make the brain ahead of time so students could move more quickly? Massimo Banzi (below) and David Cuartielles worked with others to build a computer brain. They named it Arduino after an early king of Italy.

It's easy to get started creating your own Arduino projects.

Web site (*http://arduino.cc*). We are here to get you started with an Arduino. So read on, do something awesome, and show your friends!

Chapter 2

Powering Inventions with Open Source

Tools such as the Arduino are allowing more people to learn about electronics and computer programming than ever before. You don't have to be a programming expert or an electrical engineer to use an Arduino. It is especially good for:

- artists who want to make interactive art (imagine a sculpture that plays a tune when you clap your hands!);
- fashion designers (what if your sweatshirt could display your heartbeat in blinking lights?);
- robot builders (do you want to make a robot that shoots flames and then puts out its own fires?);
- and people who are just learning to use technology.

In other words, the Arduino is for you.

When visiting the Arduino Web site, you will see the words "open source." Generally, open source means that everything about the project is available

If you want to learn more about computers, Arduino programming is a great way to start.

for everyone to look at and use. From the electronic designs used to build the physical device to the **code** used to write the software, it's all free for others to see, take, and tweak.

Making your project open source often makes it a lot easier for people to fix problems. Anyone can help with an open-source project. This helps build a better project, and knowledge is more easily spread for other projects. If someone makes your project better or useful in a new way, the options grow for everybody.

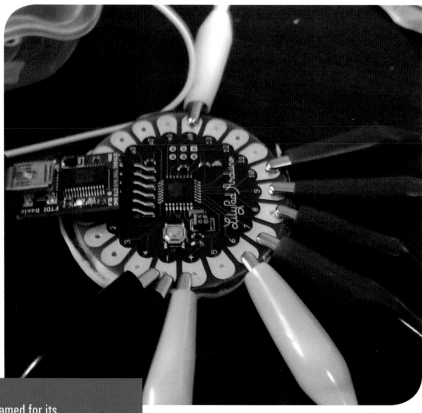

The LilyPad Arduino was named for its round shape.

Three Arduino Creators

What do people make with an Arduino? Let's take a look at three creators!

Sebastián Alegría

After his home in the South American country of Chile was hit by a terrible earthquake, Sebastián Alegría wanted a better way to find out when a quake was happening. Alegría combined his Arduino, a movement-sensing device he bought at a local store, and Twitter into a new invention. His device alerts 30,000 Twitter followers when earthquakes are occurring.

RepRap 3D Printing Project

Makers often rely on 3D printers to quickly create custom tools, toys, and trinkets from plastic. When they needed a way to make their 3D printers convert designs onscreen into three-dimensional plastic objects, they used Arduinos!

Leah Buechley

Leah Buechley used Arduino's open-source code to create the LilyPad kit. The kit allows users to add lights and electronics to clothing. Buechley, a professor at the Massachusetts Institute of Technology in Cambridge, Massachusetts, leads a team that brainstorms creative ways to bring people, electronics, and making together.

Chapter 3

Getting to Know Your Arduino

Now that you know a bit about why Arduinos were invented and what you can do with them, let's start using them. First off, there are many different Arduino models. We will be using the Arduino Uno (*uno* means "one" in Italian). Let's get to know its parts.

The Arduino's USB port makes it easy to attach to another computer.

The Arduino's Brain: Atmel ATmega 328

This computer chip stores and runs the programs you create. It is the brain inside your Arduino.

USB (Universal Serial Bus) Connector

This **port** lets you plug in a cable that connects your Arduino to your computer. It provides power and transports information back and forth between your computer and the Arduino.

External Power

You can also use the external power port to plug in batteries or connect your Arduino to a wall outlet.

Power Pins

These pins let you bring power from the Arduino to electronic parts such as lights or motors.

Analog I/O Pins

These pins allow you to connect devices that will take measurements and report them back to the Arduino. This is important for connecting input devices such as light sensors.

Digital I/O Pins

These pins allow you to connect devices that send or receive two different states, either "on" (known to the Arduino as a HIGH state) or "off" (known to the Arduino as a LOW state).

These are just the most commonly used parts of the Arduino. There is a lot more to discover and learn once you've got the basics down.

In addition to the Arduino hardware, you will use Arduino sketches. These are the programs you write that tell the Arduino how it will interact with the world.

Find the Connections!

The Arduino makes it easy to invent stuff because it contains a lot of premade connections between pins, ports, and the Atmel chip. For fun, flip over the Arduino and see if you can find the traces, or wires, that connect the pins to the chip!

Once uploaded, a sketch lives inside the Atmel chip. By instructing the Arduino where to send and receive information through its 20 input (I) and output (O) pins, you can control motors, speakers, lights, and more!

The Arduino's 20 input and output pins give users plenty of options for creating complex devices.

Chapter 4

How to Communicate with Your Arduino

An Arduino needs both hardware (like an Arduino Uno) and software. We are going to use software called Arduino Development Environment, which allows us to write a sketch and upload it to the Arduino Uno.

If your computer does not already have the Arduino software, installing it will be your first mission. This will require access to the Internet. If you are not using your own computer, you'll need to get permission from the computer's owner to install software. If you have never installed software before, find someone who can show you how to do it.

Ready to install? Head over to *www.arduino.cc* and download the latest version of the Arduino software. The site has great installation instructions, so take your time with them and meet us back here after you've got your Arduino Development Environment up and running.

Speaking a New Language

Computers and people speak different languages. The code you write in your sketch may look like a strange series of commands at first, but it will become familiar over time. When you finish writing, you will verify and compile your sketch. This process translates your code from the something-like-English version that you wrote into machine language, a version of the sketch that computers can understand.

Type Carefully!

Computers can be very, very picky. You and I do a pretty good job recognizing words no matter where someone puts cApiTAL lETTErs, or if we spell sometihng wrogn. Computers can't figure out these differences, which can result in a nonworking and often noncompiling sketch. Be careful!

Once you have verified and compiled the sketch, you can use a USB cable to upload it from your computer to the Arduino. If everything goes correctly, you will see the Arduino's Receive and Transmit lights flash as your sketch uploads. This typically takes only a few seconds, but slower computers may take a minute or two to upload the sketch.

Once the upload completes, the sketch now lives inside the Atmel 328. Your sketch will start running just after the upload completes and will continue to do so until the Arduino is no longer powered. A sketch will stay in the Arduino until you decide to upload a new one. Unlike a regular computer that can store many programs, an Arduino can remember only one sketch at a time.

The steps above may be new to you, so let's use the Arduino, and see what this looks like in action.

LED Blink

The creators of the Arduino Uno created the **LED** Blink exercise to get new users familiar with the process of creating, verifying, compiling, and running a sketch. Like the Arduino hardware and software, Blink is open source. That means anyone can use, change, or publish it. It belongs to everyone!

In this exercise, you'll type in the sketch and upload it to the Arduino. If you do those steps successfully, one of the LED lights on the Arduino board should start blinking. You will need the following:

- a computer with Arduino software installed
- an Arduino (we used the Arduino Uno)
- a USB A/B cable (the kind you use to connect your computer to a printer)

Creating a blinking LED is a common project for Arduino beginners.

Launch your Arduino software. Click on the File menu. Select Examples, then select 01. Basics, and finally select Blink. Blink is one of the sample files that comes preinstalled in your Arduino software.

If you can't find it, you can start a new sketch by going to the File menu and clicking New. Then go to *http://arduino.cc/en/Tutorial/Blink*. Click on the Get Code link and select all of the sketch. Copy and paste it into the Arduino software. Look at the image on page 21. Do you see the Text Editor section? That is where your sketch should be.

Here is what the different parts of the sketch do:

void **setup**(){

This section usually tells the Arduino (and you) where devices have been plugged in, whether lights and sensors should be on (HIGH) or off (LOW) when the Arduino starts the sketch, and more. This section begins with an open curly brace: {. It ends with a

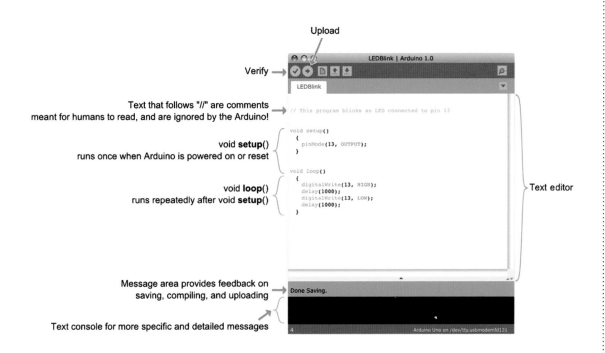

Upload

Verify →

LEDBlink | Arduino 1.0

LEDBlink

Text that follows "//" are comments meant for humans to read, and are ignored by the Arduino!

```
// This program blinks an LED connected to pin 13
```

void **setup**()
runs once when Arduino is powered on or reset

```
void setup()
{
    pinMode(13, OUTPUT);
}
```

void **loop**()
runs repeatedly after void **setup**()

```
void loop()
{
    digitalWrite(13, HIGH);
    delay(1000);
    digitalWrite(13, LOW);
    delay(1000);
}
```

Text editor

Message area provides feedback on saving, compiling, and uploading

Done Saving.

Text console for more specific and detailed messages

4

Arduino Uno on /dev/tty.usbmodemfd131

closing curly brace: }. The void **setup**() function appears at the beginning of a sketch. It runs every time your Arduino is powered on or reset.

pinMode(13, OUTPUT);}
This lets the Arduino know that you are going to use pin 13 as an output, meaning that you're going to plug something into the Arduino's pin number 13, and the

Arduino will tell the pin to do something (like blink the light). If this said INPUT, it would mean that pin 13 would be receiving information (from a light sensor or temperature sensor, for example) for the Arduino to act on. The closing curly brace notes the end of the void **setup**() function.

void **loop**(){

This section will repeat over and over again, unless you tell it otherwise. This line typically occurs right after the end of the void **setup**() function. Typically, the loop section is where the code tells the Arduino what to do.

digitalWrite(13, HIGH);

This lets the Arduino know that you're going to begin communication to a pin. The "13" tells the Arduino which pin to use, and "HIGH" allows electricity to flow to anything connected to that pin.

delay(1000);

This function lets the Arduino know you're going to pause the sketch in its current state for one second.

Arduino measures time in milliseconds, so 1,000 milliseconds, as shown here, equals one second.

digitalWrite(13, LOW);
This tells the Arduino to send a LOW value to pin 13. "LOW" often means "off."

delay(1000);}
This tells the Arduino to pause the sketch for another second. The closing curly brace indicates the end of the void **loop**() function and the end of the sketch. The sketch will now go back up to where the loop began and repeat over and over until you unplug your Arduino.

People often leave comments in a sketch that are meant for humans to read, not the Arduino. These comments begin with "//" and are followed by a phrase, like this:

//This sketch was developed by the Arduino team. The Arduino knows to ignore this text. Similarly, any text between "/*" and "*/" is ignored. Good code does not usually need many comments, but you should use them to explain important or confusing parts. They'll tell the next person who uses your code why you did what you did.

Check Your Work

Once you have pasted your sketch into the software, you want the system to check for errors. Look in the top left corner of the Arduino software window. See the checkmark? That's the Verify button. Click it! The software will now check to see if your code can compile. If everything goes well, you should see the words "Done Compiling" in the message area below the text editor. If you get an error message, it could

What's with the Colored Text?

The colored text in the Arduino code is often referred to as syntax highlighting. The Arduino Development Environment highlights certain words that it recognizes as having a specific purpose. If you see a word that is not colored although it normally is, it often means you have a misspelled word or your punctuation is incorrect. Double-check everything!

Learning to spot errors in your code is an important part of programming.

mean a few different things. Here are some common problems:

- A missing or extra curly brace {}, parenthesis (), or semicolon ;
- Incorrect spelling or punctuation

Double-check your sketch. Take a two-minute break if you get frustrated. Taking a short walk can do amazing things for resetting and refreshing your brain.

Ready to Go

Once your sketch compiles properly, it's time to move it over to the Arduino. This is called "uploading your sketch." Look for the right arrow button near the top of the window. Click it! This will begin the uploading process. If your upload is successful, you should see "Done Uploading" in the message area at the bottom of your screen, and no orange errors. You will also know that your sketch uploaded properly if you have a blinking LED on your Arduino!

Do more! Go back to the sketch and try to figure out which number indicates how long the light should be on (HIGH) and which number indicates how long the light should be off (LOW). How can you change the sketch to make the LED flash faster or slower?

If something isn't working, fixing it is usually simple. First, check that your code compiled properly when you clicked Verify. If it did not compile properly, go back and edit your sketch for errors. Try these steps if it compiled properly but you didn't get a blinking light:

Problems with Arduino projects are often caused by simple mistakes.

1. Make sure you have the right board selected under Tools -> Board. We used an Arduino Uno, so we selected Arduino Uno under the Tools -> Board menu.

2. Make sure you have the right serial port selected under Tools -> Serial. For example, we used "/dev/tty.usbmodem" on a Mac. On a Windows machine, we used the highest COM Port listed: "COM7".

3. Try uploading again! Checking the connections of your cables and devices can also help solve problems.

What will you do with your Arduino?

If you continue to have problems, the Arduino Web site has some great resources for solving common issues: *http://arduino.cc/en/Guide/Troubleshooting.*

Share What You Do with the World
Now you've been exposed to computer programming skills, electricity, circuits, and wiring—the basics of any sophisticated electrical device. Nice work! We hope you'll want to keep learning with your Arduino, so check out the resources at the back of this book—and share your awesome creations with others!

Glossary

code (KODE) text written in a computer programming language

hardware (HAHRD-wair) computer equipment, such as a printer, monitor, or keyboard

input (IN-put) information fed into a computer

LED (ELL-EE-DEE) a small light that can be switched on or off; LED stands for light-emitting diode

makers (MAY-kurz) people who invent, create, or fabricate something

output (OUT-put) the information a computer produces when it runs a program

port (PORT) a place on a computer that is designed for plugging in cables or other devices

software (SAWFT-wair) computer programs

Find Out More

BOOKS

Banzi, Massimo. *Getting Started with Arduino*. Sebastopol, CA: Make:Books/O'Reilly, 2009.

Monk, Simon. *30 Arduino Projects for the Evil Genius*. New York: McGraw-Hill, 2013.

O'Neill, Terence, and Josh Williams. *3D Printing*. Ann Arbor, MI: Cherry Lake, 2014.

WEB SITES

Instructables
www.instructables.com
Search for instructions for fun Arduino-based projects.

Sylvia's Super-Awesome Maker Show!
http://sylviashow.com
Check out some videos by a young maker who sometimes builds things using an Arduino.

Index

About the Authors

Terence O'Neill (left) works in libraries in Ann Arbor, Michigan. He loves all kinds of libraries, learning about new things, and connecting people with learning.

Josh Williams (right) is the shop manager at All Hands Active, a makerspace in Ann Arbor, Michigan. When he's not organizing workers and volunteers, or teaching classes on programming, Arduinos, and 3D printers, he spends time hiking with his wife.